Mourning

The Arts and Living

Nicholas Penny

General editors for the series John Fleming and Hugh Honour

London: Her Majesty's Stationery Office

Acknowledgements

I have received much help from the many
departments of the Victoria and Albert Museum
which I have pestered with enquiries. I am
particularly grateful to Mrs. Ginsburg of the
Department of Textiles and Dress for useful
hints. Above all, I must thank my editors Hugh
Honour and John Fleming, and my wife Anne
for the many improvements which they made to
the manuscript. This book is for Anne and for
Caroline and Elizabeth.

With the following exceptions all the objects
illustrated are from the Victoria and Albert
Museum. Fig.7 Museum of London;
Fig.21b Royal Commission on Historical
Monuments; Fig.27 British Museum.

Design by HMSO Graphic Design

ISBN 0 11 290288 X

Contents

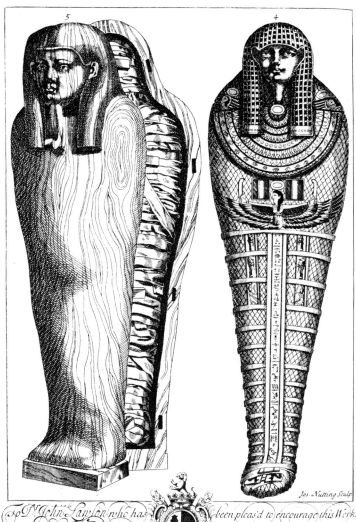

5

4

Jos. Nutting Sculp.

To Dr. John Lawson who has been pleas'd to encourage this Work, this Plate is humbly dedicated by his most humble Servant Thomas Greenhill

1 Offerings, Mummies and Vaults

Tombs are the oldest form of architecture known to us and the oldest art known to us was buried inside them. From the very earliest civilizations of which traces survive we may observe that the artist had no more important function than to support the beliefs which men seem always to have required when faced by the fact of death. We think first, perhaps, of the embalmed bodies of the rulers of ancient civilizations and when we do so most of us find it hard to feel other than remote from the civilizations who put their skills to such perverse ends, lavishing surgical and cosmetic expertise in preserving the dead instead of the living *[fig.1]*, and building pyramids instead of powerstations or hospitals *[fig.2]*. Investigation of recent burial customs may however make us feel less remote from these ancient civilizations.

In the course of this book, we will often jump from one period and civilization to another, and it is hoped that these abrupt transitions, familiar to all museum visitors, will help to shed new light on the past, and, possibly the present as well. The subject of mourning, if it was treated comprehensively, would involve some discussion of material as diverse as Attic *Stelae* and the Taj Mahal, ancestor images on Pacific Islands, the Père Lachaise, the flaming funeral ships of the Vikings, the refrigeration of the dead in California and the origins of portraiture in antiquity. But since this book is illustrated by material in the Victoria and Albert Museum, the jumps will, for the most part,

Figure 1. Two Egyptian mummies – a 'rouled' body in its wooden coffin to be seen in the 'musaeum of the Grand Duke of Tuscany' and a paste figure covered with 'Cyphers, Figures, Letters, Characters and other Hieroglyphics' to be seen in the 'musaeum of Johannes Nardius'. From Thomas Greenhill's *Art of Embalming*, London 1705.

5

Figure 2. I. Kip, An 'Ichnography' and 'schenography' of burial chambers by the Nile, not for above Memphis. From Thomas Greenhill's *Art of Embalming*, London 1705.

be made within European history of the last six or seven centuries. However, we must turn back, first of all, to early Imperial China.

The Chinese ruling class of the *Han* and *T'ang* periods (206 B.C.–221 A.D. and 618–906 A.D.) buried their dead in chambers furnished with paintings, relief carvings and lacquered timber and supplied with swords and jewellery *[pl.1]*, combs, chopsticks and bronze mirrors. In addition, tomb chambers are filled with earthenware models (*Ming Ch'i*) of domestic animals and domestic women *[pl.2 and fig.3]*, soldiers, grooms, acrobats, houses, granaries and wells. These models were magical substitutes for the real wives, servants and animals formerly immolated – a practice which Confucius had condemned as barbaric. One purpose of this series of books is to explain how 'museum objects' were once used, and to describe the social environment for which they were designed. But in the case of these objects we should remind ourselves that they were never intended for the service of the living. The comment 'What a pity it is no longer used', is, for once, hardly an apt one.

We do not, of course, now believe that the dead will be able to use any presents we give them. But we do not only give presents because the present itself will be appreciated, but to satisfy the recipient, or, it may be, to satisfy other people, or our

Figure 3. Model sheep-fold. Green-glazed earthenware, *Han.*

conscience, that we are prepared to make some sacrifice for someone we love – or respect – or fear. And this, of course, is why mourners still give presents to the dead. For they do still do so, even if only in the sense of 'giving' a funeral or laying a wreath. Such offerings are hardly akin to the practices of the ancient Chinese. And yet even in Han China a satirist could claim that the funerals given to great officials with their lavish provisions for a future life were devices for the hypocritical display of filial respect, so that even if ostensibly designed to serve the dead earthenware tomb figures might also serve to placate the conscience and impress the community of the living.

Very little is buried with the dead today, but great officers of state still throw their staffs into the monarch's grave and bishops, a century ago, might still be buried with their croziers, and peers with their coronets. The history of such 'grave gifts' is, for the most part, the history of the substitution of tokens for real offerings, In ancient China the tomb figures, themselves substitutes for real wives and chickens and so on, were replaced after the ninth century by paintings of such objects on paper which was burnt with the corpse. In the nineteenth century British adventurers discovered that nomad tribesmen still slaughtered horses to bury with their chief – in more civilized Britain a nobleman's horse would be led to his grave, but then returned to the stable. To the great distress of our colonial administrators Indian widows still, in the nineteenth century, practised *suttee*, immolating themselves on their husband's funeral pyre. The colonial administrator's own widow would not kill herself, but she would, instead, 'cut herself off' from the pleasures of life. Great warriors were once buried with their weapons: today a helmet or beret may still adorn a soldier's coffin. The crown, sceptres, rings and robes with which our medieval kings were buried were gradually replaced by imitations of less precious material, and these were, in the late middle ages, not buried, but simply displayed on the king's funeral effigy and then returned to the royal wardrobe.

When, in 1774, the Dean and Chapter of Westminster exhumed the remains of King Edward I, and the antiquaries carefully recorded the good condition of the embalmed flesh (beneath the serecloth which the king had, optimistically, ordered to be renewed every summer) and the even better condition of the crown, and of the velvet and tissue which he wore, they did not consider themselves as witnesses to the practices of 'dark and monkish times'. They would themselves have been carefully dressed for burial, although the 'Buried in Wool' Act, passed in the late seventeenth century to promote the British wool trade, exacted a fine when any other material but wool was employed.

One is reminded of the death of Narcissa in Pope's first *Moral Essay*:

> 'Odious! in woollen! 'twould a Saint provoke,
> (Were the last words that poor Narcissa spoke)
> No, let a charming chintz, and Brussels lace
> Wrap my cold limbs, and shade my lifeless face'

A concern to look one's best at the burial (or in the new life, or on the 'Great Day', or when exhumed by the archaeologist) may excite the satirist's scorn, but it must meet with hearty approval from all historians of textiles and dress. The fragments of woven silk, painted linen and tapestry from Egypt between the third and tenth century, which may be admired in the Victoria and Albert Museum, have for the most part survived because they were buried. The robes of which they were once a part no doubt sometimes corresponded to the best apparel of the living, as would have been the case with Edward I and Narcissa; but some of the fragments are decorated with scenes from the New Testament, or with images of Apollo, Orpheus or Hermes Psychopompos, the conductor of souls *[fig.4]*.

Immediately after expressing her horror at the prospect of woollen grave-clothes Narcissa asks her maid to give one cheek more rouge

> 'One would not, sure, be frightful when one's dead—'

Indeed, embalming was not a forgotten art in the eighteenth century. Thomas Greenhill in his standard apology for the practice, the *Art of Embalming* of 1705, complains that the art

Figure 4. Tapestry panels from a linen tunic decorated with the gods Hermes and Apollo. From the burial grounds at Akhmin, Egypt, 4–5th century A.D.

had been debased by the undertakers, which suggests that it was in considerable demand. The modern English distaste at the idea may perhaps be traced back to George III who is said to have given directions on the demise of his beloved daughter, Princess Amelia, that the 'barbarous practice' be dispensed with. The Prince Regent, however, on the death of Princess Charlotte in 1817 directed the Sergeant Surgeon of the King to go about his dismal business. But there was widespread disgust at this 'violation of the decent respect' due to the Princess, and it greatly distressed her widower, Prince Leopold, who was not even consulted concerning the operation! After this date embalming decreased in popularity – although it was still practised when the body of an English nobleman who died abroad was to be transported back to the security of the family vaults. Byron's letters from Italy make some grim jokes about Dr. Polidori's operations on the dead for this purpose.

The enormous importance attached to the security of family vaults may be best understood in the light of a literal belief in the resurrection of the body. Whilst waiting for this occasion it was best not to be in an alien (and un-Protestant, or, it may be, largely un-Christian) land. From this sort of thinking it is no great leap to the idea that one should keep one's 'bodily vestments' in good order against their eventual re-occupation by the soul on the Day of Judgement. This may sound like a very primitive idea, but it is the justification for embalming which we find in Greenhill. He does not deny the superior importance of the soul, but points out that we should esteem the body the more for the soul's sake 'in that it has once been in a happy state of conjunction with it, and in that it shall again be reunited therewith'. This was not, of course, the only motive – or excuse – for embalming. Certainly it was not why Bentham arranged for his own remains to be preserved at University College, London, nor why Trotter, the secretary and biographer of Charles James Fox, tried to get the great Whig leader embalmed, nor why the Russians embalmed Lenin and Stalin.

Greenhill expected his readers to share his ambition to emulate the mummies of Egypt which he illustrated *[fig.1]*. And there were also to be attempts in this country to emulate the pyramids. In 1829 publicity was given to a serious proposal to erect a London pyramid, four times as high as St. Paul's and with capacity for ten million coffins. This was a utilitarian and democratic reply to the proud isolation of the Pharoahs: more truly Egyptian in spirit if not in scale were the pyramids erected or projected for the exclusive use of an English noble family. Two designs by Sir William Chambers for mausolea of this type are preserved in the Victoria and Albert Museum, one a plain pyramid, the other adorned by urns and other ornaments. And twenty-five years after Chambers's death Bonomi erected a pyramid mausoleum for the Earl of Buckinghamshire at Blickling, Norfolk, when the family vault in the parish church was packed to capacity. Although the example of the Egyptians was important, it was the mausolea of the Romans (who had themselves, on occasions, imitated pyramids) which principally attracted the English in the second half of the eighteenth century. This is particularly clear in some of the earliest and most important projects for English mausolea – those proposed by William Chambers for Frederick, Prince of Wales not long after the prince's death in 1751.

One of Chambers's proposals survives, both in elevation, plan

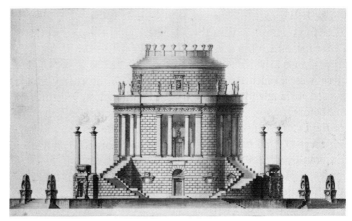

Figure 5. John Yenn, after Sir William Chambers, Elevation of a Mausoleum for Frederick Prince of Wales. Pen, ink and watercolour, probably 1752.

and section, among the Victoria and Albert Museum's drawing collection. The elevation (which is drawn by the architect's assistant John Yenn) invites comparison with the celebrated ruined mausoleum of Cecilia Metella on the Via Appia, also colossal, rusticated and with an elegant garlanded frieze *[fig.5]*. But it also recalls the imperial mausolea, such as that of Hadrian, which were known to have the upper stories set back and ringed with statues. The section shows the extraordinarily thick walls of the building by displaying it as an imaginary ruin *[fig.6]*. Even when crumbling and overgrown on the exterior, the chapel with its coffered dome and the vaults below remain in pristine condition and quite secure. This conceit of envisaging the building in ruins may well reflect Chambers's acquaintance with that most fanatical admirer of the endurance of Roman ruins, Giovanni Battista Piranesi: indeed in both erudition and extravagance the project seems indebted to Piranesi's early etchings. But although there are oddities here (such as the egg-like porphyry urns nestling in the stumpy obelisks) Chambers could never have disregarded decorum in the way Piranesi so often did.

The Dowager Princess Augusta did not carry out Chambers's plans for a mausoleum. Wren's magnificent project of over half a century earlier for a mortuary chapel for Charles I and the Stuart kings at Windsor likewise remained only on paper. And there was in fact no royal mausoleum or mortuary chapel erected in England after Henry VII's chapel at Westminster and before the small one erected by Queen Victoria at Frogmore for the Duchess of Kent, which was soon followed by the large one there erected for herself and Albert. George III, however, did employ James Wyatt to construct a proper vault for his family at Windsor, well ventilated, of impregnable masonry, and furnished with central slabs for Kings and Queens and side shelves for the others. It was nothing to compare with the marmorial splendours of the Spanish royal vault at the Escorial which William Beckford, at one time, had wanted Wyatt to recreate for him at Fonthill. But it was impressive. And in 1861, when Prince Albert's coffin was temporarily laid to rest there, the newspapers breathlessly reported on the bright silver plates

Figure 6. Sir William Chambers, Section of a Mausoleum for Frederick Prince of Wales, imagined as a ruin. Pen, ink and watercolour, February 1752.

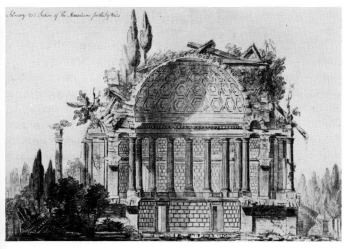

and handles and the perfect velvet of the Hanoverian coffins and how nothing, not even dust, had 'soiled their funereal grandeur'.

But by 1861 the ideas of the impregnable and immaculate vault was much less admired than formerly. In the early part of the century more and more of the middle classes had aspired to obtain church vaults–the remains of Anna Rhodes, we read in the inscription of her monument, occupied the forty-second vault of the chapel in which she was buried *[fig.25]* – but these vaults rapidly became overcrowded and, even when secure against body snatchers and lead thieves, they were insanitary. Need for more space and concern for hygiene led to the foundation of new landscaped suburban cemeteries for the upper and middle classes, and although these at first included catacombs, the belief of one of the pioneers of such cemeteries, John Claudius Loudon, that

'piling up musty coffins in vaults is quite unsuitable to the present age, and practiced only by antiquated kings and nobles, fast dying off in every part of the world'

was soon to be widely shared – even by the kings and nobles. For those who had read the romantic poets the idea of being rolled around with earth and stones and trees was no longer repellant. And Christians questioned whether the parson who trickled a few pieces of gravel on top of a coffin in a vault was really committing 'earth to earth'. All the same, it was undeniable that Jesus Christ, as Greenhill reminded his readers, was 'far from being displeas'd at the Embalming his Body'.

2 Undertakers, Funerals and Catafalques

If there was a change of attitude to embalming and to vault burial about a century and a half ago–in this country at least–then we may attempt to trace the origins of the modern feeling that ostentatious monuments, funerals and mourning are in 'bad taste'. As far as monuments are concerned the preference for simplicity has never been rare in this country. There are cases where wealthy families have confined their church monuments to modest and uniform tablets. There are also cases where inscriptions record that the deceased expressly directed that he be commemorated only by an 'unadorned stone'. And there were no doubt others who imitated Addison's 'honest country-gentleman' (in *Spectator* Paper No.662) who charged his son in private to erect no monument, but did not publicize his humility by leaving such a direction in his will.

It is rarer, before the late nineteenth century, to find expression given to the idea that the funerals and the mourning of the great should be simple, in the modern sense. When a gentleman requested in his will that his funeral be without 'unnecessary parade and show' we should realize that considerable display was necessary for anyone of 'consequence'. Indeed it was positively irresponsible for anyone of high 'station' in life to treat their funeral as a private affair. In a royal funeral, even today, the private sentiments of the royal family are overweighed by considerations of what is due to royalty, and by the need to provide a wide public with the opportunity to pay homage to their sovereign. And this was also the case in the last century and before with a great nobleman. He would lie in state in a specially draped chamber whilst family, friends, social peers and dependents filed past. The funeral procession, involving, in the case of a prominent duke, almost all the gentlemen of a county, and perhaps thousands of tenants, would proceed through

15

villages, sometimes whole towns, closed up in mourning, with streets draped in black and muffled bells tolling. If the nobility are buried with less pomp today it is not simply because of a change of taste, but because they no longer possess a fraction of their former authority.

The grand funerals of the English nobility, had, during the sixteenth century, been organized by the College of Heralds, but during the seventeenth century the undertakers successfully challenged the College's monopoly, and by the eighteenth century the College was reduced to organizing only a handful of such funerals and playing a much smaller role than they formerly had in royal funerals. By the eighteenth century the black mourning cloak and hood had passed from fashion, yet, in spite of this, the funerals became blacker than before, for the heralds had worn brilliant colours, whereas undertakers did not; and the undertakers also introduced the fashion for nocturnal funerals, which remained popular throughout the eighteenth century, lit only by boys bearing branched candlesticks. The undertaker's mute *[fig.7]* with his draped wand replaced the herald's 'conductor' with his staff; and the mourner carrying the coronet upon a velvet cushion and the 'featherman' with a tray of nodding black plumes on his head (a remarkable invention surely mothered by a surplus), replaced the line of heralds bearing the 'hatchments' of crested helmet, sword, shield, coat of arms and coronet. 'Hatchment' now came to mean the black lozenge-shaped board upon which the arms of the deceased were painted, and which hung up on the house of the deceased for six months or a year, and thereafter in the church, where many may still be seen.

By the nineteenth century the undertakers had recognized that they could expand the market for their services and they offered modified versions of the show which they had originally designed for the nobility and gentry to the middle and lower classes. They also invested extensively in new burial grounds.

Plate 1 (opposite). A sleeve-weight for cerements (Ya-Hsiu) of entwined Phoenixes. Gitl bronze, probably *T'ang*, from a tomb in North China.

Plate 2. Tomb-figure of a lady holding a mirror. Orange and green glazed earthenware, *T'ang*, late 7th-early 8th centuries A.D. Eumorfopoulos collection.

Plate 3 (opposite). Lithograph by W. Simpson, after Louis Haghe's painting of the Lying-in-State of the Duke of Wellington at Chelsea Hospital. Published by Ackermann, 1852.

On the opposite side of the Canopy HOSTE DEVICTO, REQUIEVIT. and between

PALMA

INSC

The Most
Viscou
& of Burnha
Baron No

Knight of
Vice Admira
& Comman
and

Knight G
of
Member
& Knig
of S.
After a seri
this G
the mo
Victory
Fran

Publish'd by LAURIE & WHITTLE.

Built for the sole purpose of Conveying the I
Cathedral, for Interment, on Thursday the 9.th of J

BUCENTAURE.—TRINIDAD. and TRAFALGAR, at bottom of the Car

RUIT·FERAT

COFFIN.

...O NELSON,
...the Nile,
...y of Norfolk,
...Hilborough,

...f the Bath;
...sty's Ships
...uncan
...icily;
...ian Order
...Merit,
...f the Crescent,
...f the Order
...n° 29.1758;
...roic Services,
...iously, in
...decisive
...s of
...gar,

ORIENT

CAR

N°. 53. Fleet Street. London. Jan.° 28 1806.

Vice Admiral Lord Viscount Nelson, to S.ʰ Pauls

(* The Car is now in the Painted Hall at Greenwich Hospital.)

14.920

Plate 5. Gregorio di Allegreto, Shrine of Santa Giustina. Marble, Paduan, c.1746.

Plate 4 (previous page).
Hand-coloured engraving of Nelson's
funeral car modelled on the Victory and
designed by James Wyatt and others.
Published by Laurie and Whittle, 1806.

Plate 6 (opposite).
Gold Pendant with an
eye painted on ivory.

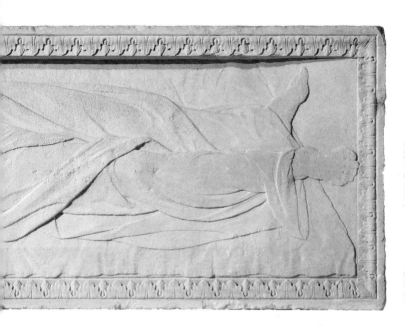

Figure 7.
The Rev. Septimus Buss,
A mute. Oil on tin,
probably 1830's.

Mr. Mold in Dickens's *Martin Chuzzlewit* is a comic version of the frightening originals interviewed by the Parliamentary Commissioners of the mid-nineteenth century. The performance stage-managed by the English undertakers seemed remarkable to foreigners. François de la Rochefoucauld describing an English funeral in 1784 adopts the same tone that the English employ today when they witness southern Italian funerals. And English funeral pomp was all the more remarkable on account of the absence of any comparable pomp in the other ceremonies of the church. Of course these funerals had their critics, such as Crabbe, in his *Parish Register* of 1807. But there is no evidence before the 1840's of widespread distaste.

During the 1840's and 1850's when the horrors of modern burial practices were investigated, the degree to which the undertakers exploited their clients and some of the ways in which their profits were made caused a national scandal. And in the same years Augustus Welby Pugin, the ardent champion of Christian – that is, Gothic – architecture, together with the high Anglican Church reformers, attacked the undertakers with unprecedented virulence. For them Mr. Mold was one of a number of highly offensive instances of the increasingly secular character of contemporary society. They would also cite 'parisien mourning rooms', and profit-making multi-denominational suburban cemeteries, fashionably landscaped and filled with pagan emblems – the pyramid, the urn, the broken column, the inverted torch.

The reformers did not confine themselves to polemics. A new style of funeral was devised, with far less emphasis on the private decoration of the hearse and much more emphasis on those fittings belonging to the church, such as hangings for the sanctuary and vestments for the clergy. They banished the mutes, plumed prancers and feathermen and they reintroduced hooded cloaks and heraldic banners (when appropriate), and much of the ancient colour – violet and blue palls, and altar frontals with red and white crosses and gold embroidery, for instance. For the poor, plain but dignified funerals were provided by enterprising clergymen who also encouraged burial clubs to become religious con-fraternities, dispensing with undertakers. Mr. Cooksey of Birmingham, a manufacturer of cheap coffins, was persuaded to work from more Christian designs *[fig.8]*.

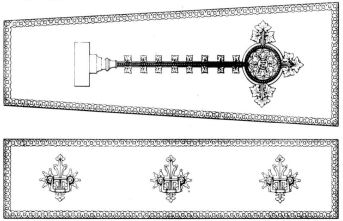

Figure 8. A cheap coffin with Christian ornaments in 'thin pliable metal' designed by G. E. Street for Cooksey of Birmingham. From *Instrumenta Ecclesiastica*, 2nd series, 1856.

Pugin and his High Anglican followers were not alone in attempting to escape from the tyranny of the undertakers in the mid nineteenth century; Prince Albert and his artistic advisers were also determined to do so when in 1852 they planned the funeral of the Duke of Wellington – certainly one of the most magnificent funerals ever seen in this country and without question better recorded than any of its competitors in magnificence (all of which are earlier in date). The duke had already lain in state at Walmer Castle where he was mourned as a duke, before he was taken to Chelsea Hospital to lie in state as a national hero, and here the undertakers (Messrs Dowbiggin and Holland) were obliged to carry out the designs of C. R. Cockerell, the Professor of Architecture at the Royal Academy. English architects had been involved on such occasions before. As Surveyor-General James Wyatt had played a prominent part in Nelson's funeral, for instance. But the effect there was not considered 'artistic' in the way that this was.

In Chelsea Hospital the hall *[pl.3]* was entirely draped in black cloth, caught up by silver cords, arranged in the diagonal pattern which Cockerell also employed in the undulating balconies of the Liverpool concert hall and in the vault of the University Library at Cambridge. Aisles leading to and from the dais were formed by rows of silver candelabra, those on the outer sides raised on pedestals modelled on antique altars, and with sentinels from the Duke's regiment standing behind them with arms reversed. The dais was surrounded by branched candelabra and the blaze of light was magically enhanced by the cloth of gold spread there and by reflectors concealed in the columns which flanked it. But to the spectators the columns appeared as bundled spears capped with plumes. They also supported the star-besprinkled black velvet which fell from the tester crowned by the ducal arms and a glory of sable banners. Below lay the coffin, topped by the ducal coronet, inside was another coffin, and inside that another coffin containing all that was mortal of the Duke.

In the case of the funeral car *[fig.9]* Messrs Banting, the Royal undertakers, had designs prepared for the Prince Consort

Figure 9. Lithograph by Day and Sons of the Duke of Wellington's Funeral car, designed by Redgrave, Semper and Hudson. published by Ackermann, 1852.

but these were not satisfactory – they were, moreover, said to have been supplied by a Frenchman – and the 'Governmental Department of Practical Art' (the parent of the Victoria and Albert Museum), was called in. Richard Redgrave, after some discussion with Henry Cole, conceived the basic idea of a six-wheeled solid bronze carriage. Professor Semper then embellished the design, rather more than Redgrave wished, with bristling trophies and dense allegorical ornament and the velvet pall, embroidered with laurels was designed by Professor Hudson 'and carried out, at least much of it, by the ladies of the School of Art'. In the solidity of the framework, and in the quality of craftmanship evident in every detail, the car was a total contrast to the imaginative but flimsy and meretricious funeral car at Nelson's funeral *[pl.4]*.

Redgrave in his *Memoirs* describes the hurry required to get the car ready in three weeks: the problem of coordinating the several founders separately casting the wheels, the reliefs of victories, the helmets, the lion heads and so on. The workmen laboured for seventy or eighty hours on end with only a few

Figure 10. Stefano Della Bella, etching of the decorations designed by Alfonso Parigi for the funeral of Francesco dei Medici in San Lorenzo, Florence. From a set of etchings bound with the book of obsequies for the Emperor Ferdinand II, 1637.

hour's sleep and were still putting the final touches to the work an hour before the twelve huge black horses, harnessed three abreast, began to tug the twenty-seven foot long vehicle to St. Paul's. These horses had to be assisted by sixty police constables when the car, which weighed eleven tons, sank into the road near the Duke of York's steps, but the cathedral was eventually reached, and the coffins buried in a Cornish granite sarcophagus, as the guns boomed from the Tower of London, and throughout Britain the parish bells were tolled.

Although Wellington's was certainly among the most magnificent funerals of the last century in Europe (it was indeed probably intended to vie in magnificence with the belated state funeral given to Napoleon Bonaparte in 1840), it can all the same hardly be compared with the funerals of European emperors, kings, princes, grand dukes and Popes, of the type which was evolved in late sixteenth century Florence and spread to other major cities by the early seventeenth century. In such funerals the entire interior, and often also the entrance façade, of a great church would be hung with mourning drapery (*panni lugubri*), and filled with coats of arms, trophies, devices, emblems and simulated marble statuary. Below the crossing there would be a catafalque for the display of the effigy, sometimes of a quasi architectural character, sometimes involving a huge stepped pyramid baldacchino ablaze with a thousand tapers, sometimes involving a baldacchino in the fashion of a tester from which drapery fell (as in Wellington's lying-in-state). These were the expected features, but novel conceits and devices were constantly introduced. Skeletons in a variety of lively attitudes (*simulacri di Morte diversamente atteggiati*) were popular in seventeenth century funeral decor, but Alfonso Parigi must have astounded the mourners for Prince Francesco de Medici in 1634 when he lined the nave of San Lorenzo in Florence with colossal skeleton knights with shields and swords and cavalier hats, and even riding horses *[fig.10]*. And Carlo Fontana must also have surprised and delighted those who attended the obsequies for Leopold I of Austria in Rome in 1705 by the cannons attended by trophy-bearing putti which he designed

Figure 11 (left). Carlo Fontana or Studio, Design for an incense cannon for the Catafalque of Leopold I of Austria, in S. Maria dell'Anima, Rome. Pen, ink and wash, 1705.

Figure 12 (right). Edward Pierce, Design for a wall monument to Diana, Lady Warburton (d.1694), erected in St. John's, Chester, with some minor modifications. Pen, ink and wash.

for the catafalque. These, as Allan Braham has shown, shot incense into the church *[fig.11]*. Later in the eighteenth century the most celebrated catafalques were probably those designed by Michel-Ange Slodtz and Charles Michel-Ange Challe in France which were admired partly for the absence of such grotesque wit.

Such ephemeral decorations of plaster and wood had an important impact on the designs of durable sepulchral sculpture. For instance, the skeletons writing in books, carrying medallions and brandishing hour-glasses in Bernini's tombs were derived from skeletons which had been similarly employed in funeral decor. A design for a tomb by the English sculptor Edward Pierce *[fig.12]* showing a skeleton holding up a shroud, upon which the epitaph was to be written (a design carried out with some modifications in St. John's, Chester) looks as if it was directly inspired by funeral decor. However, in England, with the single glorious exception of the catafalque designed by Inigo Jones for the funeral of James I, such funeral decor was not to be seen. It was not appropriate to protestant, constitutional monarchs. But whilst the Hanoverians were buried with relatively little ceremony the exiled Stuarts were accorded extravagant honours. The catafalque of James II of 1702 in S. Lorenzo in Lucina, Rome, designed by Sebastiano Cipriani *[fig.13]* was followed in 1766 by that of James III in SS. Apostoli, Rome, designed by Aptici, with less art, but no less pomp.

Figure 13. Engraving by Specchi of the catafalque of King James II of England designed by Sebasiano Cipriani for S. Lorenzo in Lucina, Rome. From C. d'Aquino, *Sacra Exequalia in Funere Jacobi II*, 1702.

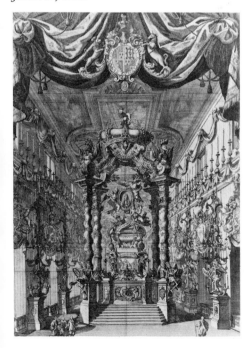

3 Shrines, Relics and Effigies

The imposing funerals of the English nobility conducted the body to a vault in the parish church, and the elaborate catafalques of European princes were erected inside great city churches. Christians had at first only permitted the burial of saints inside their places of worship, but the more powerful members of the congregation gradually sought burial near the shrines of the saints and, by the middle ages, the laity were commonly buried in the religious buildings which they founded or endowed. Eventually, in England, the Church opened her vaults to anyone who could afford them (even, as has already been mentioned, to Miss Anna Rhodes), although in Catholic countries, especially those with hot climates, this privilege was limited to ecclesiatics and the most exalted of the laity. The tombs of saints are then the oldest form of christian monument. They remain the most important. Sometimes, the shrine resembles an ordinary altar – but with the embalmed body visible, through crystal, inside. Sometimes there is a sculptured effigy of the saint in place of the embalmed body: Maderna's St. Cecilia below the High Altar of St. Cecilia in Trastevere in Rome is the most famous example of this. An earlier example of this type of sculpture is the relief of Santa Giustina by Gregorio di Allegreto *[pl.5]* which is probably to be identified as a part of the 'Archam Lapideam Ornatum' ordered by the Consiglio of Padua, to be constructed 'de novo' in 1476, but which was never, it seems, used to receive the saint's body. Instead it served, eventually, as a water trough, and there is an ugly overflow hole bored through one side of the sarcophagus damaging the relief of an angel.

Although now displayed at a level with our eyes this relief may have been intended to be placed below an altar, and the perspective makes more sense when thought of in this way.

Exceptionally good light would however be needed if the sweet disorder of the saint's hair and of the tassels of her cushion and the variations in the fluent rhythms of the drapery folds, which are carved in very low relief, were to be appreciated.

The sculptor of this work is to be identified only because of the similarity between this effigy and those of Paduan tombs which are known to be his, and were it not for the nimbus and diadem we would suppose that this was an ordinary tomb effigy rather than the image of a saint. Tombs in the late middle ages, especially when chantries were established around them, came very close to shrines in appearance, and although one prayed in a chantry for the soul of the deceased, whereas at a shrine one prayed to a saint, Queen Elizabeth I was conscious that in protecting old tombs from the fury of iconoclasts she was liable to be accused of nourishing a 'kinde of superstition'. There is, of course, an obvious relationship between the veneration of the mourner and of the worshipper – a point sharply made by Thomas Tenison in his treatise *Of Idolatry* of 1678 in which he remarked that if one believed that religious imagery was no help in exciting 'memory and passion' then one imputed 'less to a crucifix than to the Tomb of our friend, or to a thread on our finger'.

Tenison's reference to mourning rings is particularly telling because mourning jewellery has for centuries (although not in our century) involved the preservation of a relic of the deceased. Although there was a scheme in Revolutionary France (when the revival of cremation was much proposed) for the ashes of the deceased to be fashioned into vitrified medallion portraits for presentation to the mourners, a lock of hair is the only part of the dead person's body, which, as a rule, we find retained as a relic. With saints it is different – larger jewelled containers being divised for their heads or hearts or limbs *[fig.14]*. There are secular equivalents to these practices: the hands of geniuses such as Galileo, Descartes or Canova are separately venerated; and in Victorian England marble replicas of the hands and arms of deceased children were cherished by protestants who had nothing but contempt for Roman Catholic relics.

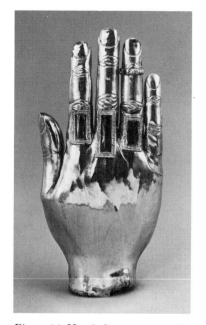

Figure 14. Hand, from an arm reliquary. Silver, parcel-gilt, Flemish, 13th century.

Figure 15. Pendant containing the hair of Charles I.

One gold pendant of about 1800 in the Victoria and Albert Museum has, on the reverse of the 'relic' of hair, not a whole face, as was quite common, but simply an eye, painted on ivory – a domestic adaptation of one of the most arresting devises of devotional art, the disembodied eye of God *[pl.6]*. An earlier example of a mourning pendant in the same collection can be described as a true reliquary, for it contains some of the hair of Charles I, king and martyr *[fig.15]*.

One obvious respect in which a tomb differs from a shrine is of course that a saint could not erect his own shrine whereas it was common practice for the great to erect their own tombs, either preparing them in their own lifetime, or charging their heirs to complete them, and it was also common, at least before

Figure 16. School of London, Recumbent effigy of a Knight of the De Lucy family, formerly in the Lady Chapel, Lesnes Abbey, Kent. Reigate sandstone, with gesso and some traces of painting and gilding, about 1320–1340.

the nineteenth century, to bequeath mourning rings, whereas no Saint could make arrangements for the distribution of his or her relics. We cannot prove that the decapitated effigy of a knight of the De Lucy family once in Lesnes Abbey in Kent *[fig.16]* was erected by the knight himself, nor can we prove that this was the case with the effigy of a knight once in a Venetian church *[fig.17]* – to cite two notable examples of fourteenth century sepulchral sculpture in the Victoria and Albert Museum – because in neither case do we know who is commemorated, but it would be unusual if they were not.

The recumbent posture which we find in both of these effigies did not pass out of fashion with the gothic. The tomb effigies by Gregorio di Allegreto, as well as his Santa Giustina, are recumbent, and so are those by most other fifteenth century

Figure 17. Paolo di Jacobello delle Masegne, Recumbent effigy of a knight. Istrian stone, Venetian, about 1370–1375.

sculptors. The posture remained popular in England as late as the seventeenth century, and we find it employed by Nicholas Stone, whom John Physick has identified as the sculptor of the magnificent double tomb to Sir Moyle Finch and his wife, Elizabeth Countess of Winchilsea, removed a few years ago from the derelict Eastwell Church, Kent *[pl.7]*. The effigies here are clearly portraits, which was not likely to have been the case with the Venetian knight (whose face is nevertheless not without expression) or with the knight from Lesnes Abbey. Stone has carved the wrinkles on the countesses face just as he has carved the buttons and pleats of her clothes, and the countess must have known that he had done so, for the tomb was erected by her in 1628, eight years before her own death and fourteen after the death of Sir Moyle, her husband, whose eyes, unlike her's, are closed. There are small holes in her head for a coronet to be fitted over her widow's coif. Her husband was made a baronet in 1611 and was in line for a peerage at the time of his death. His widow worked hard to become Viscountess Maidstone, and, later, Countess of Winchilsea, and she would have been upset that her effigy should lack this crowning glory.

The tomb is also, in other, more important respects, the shadow of its original self. Sockets in the marble base show where an iron railing would once have been fitted. The eight bases remind us that there were originally columns of touchstone carrying a canopy adorned with putti, strapwork, inscriptions, and huge heraldic achievements. Around the alabaster tombchest are the names of twelve children of this couple, and when the children are so named in other monuments of this period, they are carved kneeling in front of their names (those who predeceased their parents, holding skulls). There would be room for such kneeling effigies here, but if they were intended it is unlikely that they were ever executed, because they do not appear in an early drawing of the monument. The heraldic devices on the monument would of course have been painted, but even without that, the monument has plenty of colour, for the tombchest of alabaster is inset with panels of a streaky serpentine. The effigies, however, are of carrara marble. The early seventeenth century was the first period in which this material was imported into England in any quantity, and it was perhaps too costly to be used for the tombchest as well as the effigies. The small pieces used in the pavement around the chest could be waste from the blocks used for the figures.

The recumbent posture was still in favour in the last decades of the seventeenth century when John Dwight portrayed his dead five year old daughter Lydia in this way (as an earthenware portrait, not a effigy) and it was employed by William Stanton in some of his tombs, such as that of Lady Rebecca Atkins in St. Paul's Church, Clapham *[figs.18 and 19]*. But other attitudes, which had been first introduced during the Renais-

Figure 18 (left). John Dwight, portrait of his dead daughter, Lydia. Stoneware, Fulham Factory, c.1674.

Figure 19 (right). William Stanton, Terracotta model for the effigy of Lady Rebecca Atkins in St. Paul's Clapham, c.1689.

Figure 20. William Stanton, Design for a monument to Dorothy, Lady Brownlow (d.1700) in St. Nicholas, Sutton, Surrey. Pen, ink, and wash.

sance, were quite as popular, and for grand tombs, reclining effigies were more common than recumbent ones. The reclining pose is a natural enough position, as effortlessly assumed by cricketers in Victorian photographs as by antique river gods, and medieval artists used the pose on occasions, for instance for Jesse below his tree and for St. Anne in the Nativity of the Virgin; but they did not use the pose for their effigies. One reason for the adoption of the reclining pose may be illustrated by the effigy of the Venetian knight *[fig.17]* which is from a high wall tomb and so is both larger than life and also tilted so that it would be clearly visible from below. The tilting makes the figure appear comically precarious and sculptors must have welcomed the reclining pose as an alternative solution. It would also be interesting to know more about the relationship between tomb effigies and the ways in which bodies or wax and wooden effigies were displayed at funerals. In England the decline of recumbent effigies in tombs coincides with the decline of the funeral effigy, a decline which is clearly indicated by contemporary comment on the eccentricity of the Duchess of Buckingham having such an effigy in the early eighteenth century.

We have seen that William Stanton designed a recumbent effigy for a freestanding tomb, but in his wall tomb for Dorothy Lady Brownlow, in St. Nicholas's, Sutton, Surrey, the deceased is shown 'lolling upon cushions' *[fig.20]*. There are, in addition, a pair of flaming urns, and five full, fat, soft putti–two upon the pediment, two, in floods of tears, at her feet where a skull is placed, and one other drawing her attention to a cluster of cherubim in a glory above. The reverie, from which this latter putto attempts to arouse Lady Brownlow, looks like the boredom of the idle rich, and although this was obviously not Stanton's intention, it is not simply a modern reaction to this style of monument. An early eighteenth century poet writes of a new style of effigy 'stretched in careless pride'. But it was the Victorians who concealed the monument behind an organ – so that it is now only possible to study it in the drawing. They may have noticed that Lady Brownlow's dress displays her figure to advantage.

4 Portraits and Mourners in Marble

However worldly we find Stanton's Brownlow monument we
cannot deny that it is religious in theme; the deceased is
awakened from her melancholy to the prospect of heavenly
glory. But there is no religious reference whatever in Michael
Rysbrack's magnificent monument to the 2nd and 3rd Dukes
of Beaufort, a work signed in 1754 and erected in 1766 at
Badminton, Gloucestershire. The sculptor's drawing for this
monument *[fig.21a]* differs in some details from the work as
eventually executed *[fig.21b]*, but in both cases the narrative
enacated is the same. It was of course an important consequence
of the 'activation' of the effigy in the Renaissance that narrative
became possible in tomb sculpture. Here the 'High, Puissant,
and most Noble Prince Henry Somerset', the 2nd duke,
reclines, holding the medallion portrait of his second wife, and
turning to his eldest son, Henry, who succeeded him as duke,
and who is standing beside his father on the massive gadrooned
sarcophagus of 'portor' marble. The heroic cast of the figures
should not conceal from us that this is an idealized *tableau* of an
essentially domestic sense. The 2nd duke discourses solemnly to
his heir on the topic of the portrait which he holds, a portrait of
the young man's mother who died when he was still an infant.
The monument, in fact, is, in a sense, about mourning.

It is hardly possible today to conceive of mourning without
portraiture; yet portraiture, as we know it, was invented, or
rather rediscovered, in the Renaissance, and the majority of
medieval effigies are not portraits at all. It is in the Renaissance
that the bust, either in the round, or in relief on a medallion, as
in Rysbrack's monument, was reintroduced into the design of
tombs. Such busts when they were for domestic use reflect the
ancient Roman custom of venerating the effigies of ancestors.
Moreover a high percentage of the earlier Renaissance busts are

Figure 21a (left). Michael Rysbrack, Preliminary design for a monument to Henry Somerset, 2nd Duke of Beaufort, Rachel, his second wife, and their son, Henry, the 3rd Duke (d.1745). Pen, ink and grey wash and yellow body colour.
21b (right). The completed monument, Marble (white statuary and *Portor*), signed 1754, erected 1766, in St. Michael's, Badminton, Gloucestershire.

posthumous portraits and thus are monuments, even if not tombs. The popularity of such busts is clearly connected by Vasari with the practice of making death masks and many of the busts clearly reflect their origin as such masks–none more so than the late quattrocento terracotta bust of an aged member of the Capponi family, perhaps Niccolo di Giovanni Capponi *[fig.22]*. Those busts of the period which are not posthumous – especially those of unbeautiful men – were often also intended for posterity, as effigies which would look down on heirs and successors. And the heirs and successors could look up with admiration – metaphorically, but also literally, for Vasari (in his life of Verrocchio) mentions that such busts were

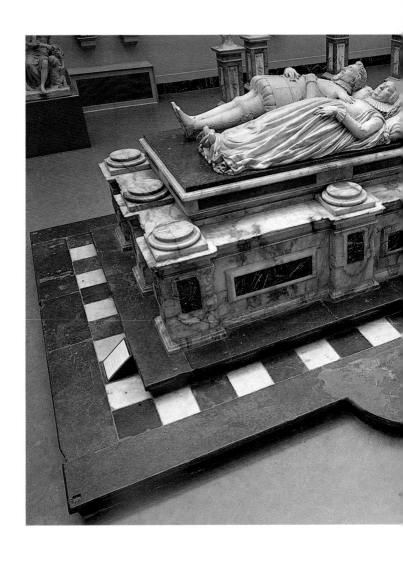

Plate 7.
Nicholas Stone, Tomb of Sir Moyle Finch, and his
wife, Elizabeth, Countess of Winchelsea, Marble,
alabaster, touch and serpentine, erected 1628 in
Eastwell Church, Kent.

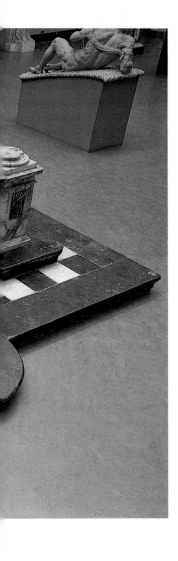

Plates 8 and 9.
Wax portraits of V. Francoschina, Italian? 17th century.
8. (top) : At 18 years of age.
9. (bottom) : At 80 years of age.

Plate 10.
Richard Cosway, miniature portrait
of Mary Russell mourning for her mother. 1786.
Lent by Mr. F. E. Perowne.

Plate 11.
Locket or brooch, showing a
willow tree and an urn.
Late 18th century.

Plate 12 (below).
Edwin Landseer, *The Old
Shepherd's Chief Mourner.*
Oil, shown at the Royal Academy
1837. Sheepshanks Collection.

Mourning for
Princess Charlotte

EVENING DRESS.

E. 3099-1888.

Plate 14. Richard Redgrave, *The Governess*. Oil, signed and dated 1844, and shown at the Royal Academy 1845 with the text 'she sees no kind domestic visage here' in the catalogue.

Plate 13 (opposite). Fashion plate showing mourning evening dress, from *La Belle Assemblée*, November, 1817.

Figure 22.
Bust of member of the
Capponi family. Terracotta
(from a death mask),
Florentine, late 15th century.

displayed 'in every house . . . over chimneypieces, doors, windows and cornices'.

The idea of a portrait of the deceased as something upon which we look with fondness remains familiar, but the idea of a portrait which looks down at us, and up to which we look – the idea of a portrait which has an active moral effect on us, is less common today. Certainly the idea of a portrait which is deliberately designed to disturb is alien to us. But that is the purpose of a pair of small coloured wax portraits, nearly four inches high, Italian and probably seventeenth century, which can still cause visitors to the Victoria and Albert Museum to shudder *[pls.8 and 9]*. One shows a young girl with elaborate coiffure, holding flowers with one hand, as do courtesans in the paintings of Palma and Titian, and pressing a naked breast with the other hand. The other portrait shows the same person, 'V. Franceschina', but aged eighty instead of eighteen, a gap-toothed hag holding a skull, and with the nipple of her now pendulous breast caught on her admonishing forearm – a nasty variant on the theme of Giorgione's *La Vecchia* (surely itself a pendant).

The contemplation of these images may have been a spiritual exercise for the sitter. Or were they meant as an unkind gift to a flighty young relation? They were surely intended to turn the

48

mind from vanity and to prepare it for physical decay and death. A similar message was to be read in many late medieval tombs, where the body is shown as a skeleton half clad in parchment-like skin perforated by busy worms. Death was also considered by the Church as a heaven-sent opportunity for frightening the worldly into a more religious frame of mind. The skulls and skeletons in Baroque monuments represent Death, not the dead, but are powerful discomforters of a related type *[fig.12]*.

By the second half of the eighteenth century educated people were quite as discomforted as ever at the idea of decay and death, but they were likely to be less sure than before that they would 'meet their maker' and less sure of the very existence of a 'future state'. In such an intellectual atmosphere grim spiritual exercises lost much of their point and both skulls and skeletons became less popular in the design of tombs. The most popular elegy of this period, certainly in England, and perhaps in Europe, was Gray's *Elegy written in a Country Churchyard*, and it differs from earlier popular elegies in that the 'trembling hope' of the Christian is invoked only briefly in the last lines, whereas the idea that we survive in the memory of affectionate mourners is central to the poem:

> On some fond breast the parting soul relies,
> Some pious drops the closing eye requires;
> E'en from the tomb the voice of Nature cries,
> E'en in our Ashes live their wonted Fires.

And it was this idea that Dr. Johnson noted as a novel one in poetry. It soon became exceedingly commonplace. Survival in the memory of those who love us is hardly an 'afterlife' compared with that offered by Christianity, and we know that gradually the 'tender pilgrimage' to the new grave will cease, the grass will grow long, and, in the words of Thomas Hood, there 'may be then'

> No resurrection in the minds of men.

But even so, that tender pilgrimage can be made into an enduring image, and so it was, over and over again, by the sculptors during the hundred years following Gray's *Elegy*.

49

Mourning figures had played an important role in late medieval monuments – a moving example being the woman leaning against the helmet at the feet of the early sixteenth century effigy of Don Garcia Osorio *[fig.23]* – but the role, if important, was still subordinate. Rysbrack, in the mid eighteenth century, could make mourning the theme of his monument to the Dukes of Beaufort. Artists of the following generations would be far more inclined to show the Dukes bent in tearful lamentation over the medallion portrait than discoursing so solemnly. The most popular convention of all was of course that of the mourner, usually female, drooping over, or beside, an urn. One finds this in painting, for instance in Richard Cosway's miniature portrait of Mary Russell mourning at her mother's urn *[pl.10]*, as well as in monuments such as that to Sir William Hillman 'of his Majesty's board of green Cloth' *[fig.24]*. Sir William died in 1793 and the monument was signed in 1800 by 'Coade and Sealy', the manufacturers of artificial stone who employed several of the leading English

Figure 23. Detail of the tomb of Don Garcia Osorio, formerly in the Church of S. Pedro Ocana, near Aranjuez. Marble, Spanish (Toledo), first quarter of the 16th century.

sculptors of the late eighteenth century. The fine, sharp detailing reflects the taste of John Bacon the elder, the chief sculptor employed, and is also an effective advertisement for the quality of the firm's moulds, for such pieces were cast, although in some cases hand finished as well, before baking. We learn from the epitaph that this monument was erected by the will of Sir William's sister. And this provides us with another clue as to why mourners are so frequently the chief subject of monuments erected after about 1750.

After that date it becomes rare for a monument to be erected during the lifetime of the person commemorated. Indeed, the practice was disapproved of and J. F. Moore's monument to Mrs. Macauley, erected in St. Stephen's, Walbrook in the 1770's was taken down at the insistence of the parishioners for this reason. It also became rarer for monuments to be commissioned by the person commemorated, and since they tended, instead, to be commissioned by mourners, the emphasis on mourning is understandable. We must not, however, suppose that the mourners can be easily identified. If the figure in Sir William's monument is meant for his sister then it is a very generalized portrait. She is quite as conventional a figure as the stylized willow trees which droop over urns in more modest tablets, and gravestones and mourning jewellery of the same period. In mourning lockets and brooches these trees can sometimes even be fashioned from a lock of hair; the urn may be adorned with tears in the form of seed pearls *[pl.11]*.

Although the mourning female figure on a monument is sometimes to be identified as the person who erected the monument, it may also be intended for a personified Virtue. 'It is a great compliment, methinks, to the sex', observes Cynthio in Addison's *Dialogue on Medals*, 'that your virtues are generally shown in petticoats.'

I can give no other reason for it, says Philander, but because they chanced to be of the feminine gender in the learned languages.

Virtues appear on the monument of Anna Rhodes, who died in 1796, by Bacon the younger, from the same Church as the

Figure 24 (left). Coade and Sealy, monument to Sir William Hillman, (d.1793), formerly in St. James', Hampstead Rd, London. Artificial stone, 1800. Lent by the London Diocesan Fund.

Figure 25 (right). John Bacon the Younger, monument to Anna Rhodes (d.1796), formerly in St. James', Hampstead Rd, London. Marble, c.1800. Lent by the London Diocesan Fund.

Hillman monument *[fig.25]*. In the top section of this Justice and Clemency embrace, the former holding scales, and with a sword at her feet, the latter with a scroll inscribed 'Pardon', and behind there is a cross with the words 'Justitia Clementia Conjuncte'. In the case of Flaxman's monument to Captain James Walker and Captain Richard Beckett erected in St. Peter's, Leeds, in 1812, the plaster model for which is preserved in the Victoria and Albert Museum *[fig.26]*, it is a female Victory who mourns these warriors who fell at the Battle of Talavera. Whereas Bacon charms us with pretty detail, Flaxman commands our attention with a design of breathtaking lucidity–the curve of Victory's nude back and the curve of her wings are both echoed and answered by the palm tree; the diagonal of the banners meets the line of her legs and arm at a right angle. As an examplar of deeply felt but quiet, dignified grief, it is an image which could not be surpassed.

Figure 26. John Flaxman, Plaster sketch model for the monument to Captain James Walker and Captain Richard Beckett, erected St. Peter's, Leeds, 1812. Lent by university College, London.

5 Suits of Woe

Unquestionably the most famous representation of grief for the dead in the Victoria and Albert Museum is Landseer's painting *The Old Shepherd's Chief Mourner [pl.12]* in which an inconsolable sheepdog keeps vigil over his master's coffin. The dog may be the chief, but he is not – as one might sentimentally suppose – the only mourner, because he can hardly have strewn the willow on the coffin. Spectacles rest on the Bible, and these would surely be a surprising possession for a shepherd much before the nineteenth century – as would a coffin for that matter – and so this was meant as a contemporary scene. All the same the picture concerns the honest simple life (and death) of those who are geographically, if not historically, as remote from the sophisticated Academy visitors of 1837 for whom the picture was painted, as from us today. In this respect it resembles Joseph Wright's painting of a young and inconsolable red Indian widow, which enjoyed success half a century earlier.

In spite of the popularity of Landseer's picture, most popular images of mourners portray domestic women rather than domestic animals – and this applies to painting no less than to sculpture. Before the woman drooping by an urn became an overwhelmingly popular subject in art, portraits of widows greatly moved the men that beheld them. Jonathan Richardson the elder wrote of Van Dyck's lost half-length portrait of the Dowager Countess of Exeter *[fig.27]*:

There is such a Benignity, such a Gentile, Becoming Behaviour, such a Decent Sorrow, and Resignation Express'd here, that a Man must be very Insensible that is not the better for considering it. The Mourning Habit excites Serious Thoughts, which may produce Good Effects. But what I confess I am particularly affected with, I who (I thank God) have for many Years been happy as a Husband, is the Circumstance of Widowhood. Not that it gives me Sorrow as remembering the Conjugal Knot must be cut, but I Rejoice that it yet subsists.

Figure 27. W. Faithorne, after A. Van Dyck, *Frances Brydges, Dowager Countess of Exeter.* Engraving.

Since it is so satisfactory for men to see women mourn it is no doubt not coincidental that it is on women that the burden of mourning almost entirely falls, and this was especially obvious in the last century when men wore dark clothes whether or not they were in mourning. There seems never to have been a male equivalent to the veil or to the 'barbe' or 'peak' or 'Marie Stuart Cap' which widows have been, at various times, obliged to wear. The anxiety which lies behind the idealization of woman as mourner is found in comedies and picaresque novels where widows are notoriously disloyal to the memories of their dead husbands, and often dangerously predatory upon unsuspecting males such as Mr. Pickwick. Leslie's painting of Uncle Toby innocently entering the web of widow Wadman *[fig.28]* is a typical genre subject; tender, it is true, but also grotesque: in high art we see the Andromaches and Agrippinas.

Figure 28. C. R. Leslie, *Widow Wadman and my Uncle Toby*, oil, shown at the Royal Academy 1831 with a quotation from Sterne's *Tristam Shandy*. Sheepshanks Collection.

The ways in which mourning once affected every aspect of life is hard for us to imagine today. It extended not only to all major articles of dress but to accessories such as parasols and handkerchiefs. There was mourning writing paper (not confined to announcements of a death) and even mourning tea services. And such extremes as the latter were not exclusively Victorian: Cunnington and Lucas in their *Costume for Births, Marriages and Deaths* cite a mid seventeenth century reference to mourning night-caps, sweet bags and combs. Eileen Harris's *Going to Bed*, in this series, mentions the special black firetongs and shovel one might find in the death chamber.

When a member of the Royal family died everyone with any social pretensions went into public mourning, and private mourning extended beyond the family, into the servant's hall and the tenant's cottages, and also into the nursery. Queen Victoria in 1859 was quite shocked that her five-month old grand-daughter in the Prussian Court nursery was not in mourning for her great grandmother. She proposed 'white and lilac' as suitable colours for the baby and 'grey or white or drab' for the nurses. Black, in fact, was by no means the only colour involved in mourning, although from the late Middle Ages it has certainly been the chief colour. There are records of purple mourning, and white was often worn, for spinsters and bachelors, and above all for children, at whose funerals white gloves and scarves and hatbands would be dispensed, white feathers seen on the hearse, and even white velvet on the coffin.

For most women, and no doubt many widows, 'the very deepest appliances of external mourning' could easily be 'rendered subservient to the exhibition of vanity.' Mourning could indeed be as fashionable as any other form of dress, although this was most obviously the case when the mourning was for royalty, rather than for a relative or friend. '. . . the head of taste is declined', gushed *La Belle Assemblée* shortly after the death of Princess Charlotte,

and the tints of varied hue no longer animate with brilliant colouring the splendid robe, or flowering coronet of Britannia's beauteous daughters.

'Yet', the next paragraph opens,

Yet Fancy and Invention never die; they watch with keen and scrutinizing eye how to give diversity even to the sable hue of solemn black, and to mingle variety even with the solemn drapery of mourning.

On this particular occasion ear pendants of jet reached new and daring lengths *[pl.13]*.

Nevertheless, we must not underestimate the penitential character of mourning conventions. Mrs. Sherwood in *The Fairchild Family* describes the eight day's wait before a funeral in a large house entirely shuttered on all sides save that which 'looked into the court of offices'. By the light permitted on that side the servants busied themselves 'renewing' the family's supply of 'crapes and bombazines, love ribbons' – a transparent silk for the decoration of hats – 'and mourning muslin'. Mrs. Tilney, a garrulous maid, remarks to one of the children that in the old days

I can assure you, when a death occurred in a family, it was a very serious business; but it is not so now, I am thankful to say.

This is because modern borders could easily be 'quilled' whereas 'formerly' (that is, probably, before the 1830's) every inch had to be broad hemmed. In addition to the gloom, the expense and the hard work for Mrs. Tilney, there was the social isolation which was involved. The ambiguous social position of the nineteenth-century governess must always have been re-inforced by clothes, which, although not those of a servant, were poorer and plainer than those of the family to which she was 'attached' as an inferior (although equal in education). But in Richard Redgrave's painting of 1844 mourning costume makes the governess, who has been forced no doubt by the death of the family breadwinner to leave home at a tender age, particularly pathetic in her isolation *[pl.14]*.

It was of course the widow who carried the greatest burden. The eyes of the 'world' were upon her, that is, upon her clothes. In general, a hundred years ago, deep mourning would be worn by the widow for a year and a day (the extra day was presumably required because the anniversary of the death would not have been an appropriate day upon which to make any change). During this period also, and usually for longer, the veil for outdoors, the widow's cap for indoors, and 'weeper' cuffs were *de rigueur*. There would then follow a year of modified mourning (sometimes in two stages) in which the special materials devised for deep mourning such as bombazine, cypress and silverets (mixtures of silk and wool or silk and linen), crape (a specially treated and textured silk), and shammy for gloves and shoes would be less dominant. All these materials were dull black, reflecting no lights, but in the second and third stages silk and some jewellery was permitted. And after the second year one could go into half-mourning, and come out of black. Thereafter one could – if one dared – move very gradually and tactfully towards bright colour. Richard Redgrave's painting *Preparing to throw off her Weeds* shows the deliberations before this step was taken *[fig.29]*.

Figure 29. Richard Redgrave, *Preparing to throw off her Weeds*, oil, shown at the Royal Academy 1846. Sheepshanks Collection.

More obviously than is the case with the other forms of dress, mourning is a form of language – or at least was one. The length of time decreed by one court for mourning a foreign prince could be read by diplomats as an index of esteem. And the degree as well as the duration was important. Were gloves to be of beaver, or shammy or lamb? Were swords to be black, were buckles to be covered, was jewellery permitted? The width of a Victorian mourning hatband and the number of tucks in mourning crape were liable to the most subtle exegesis. But some things were quite clear. For instance, to the original admirers of Redgrave's *Governess [pl.14]*, or of the earlier and more painful version of the picture where the young lady is only a poor teacher, it would have been clear that her father (or guardian) died at least three months ago, because that was the period prescribed for first mourning for members of the family, and she is now wearing silk and therefore in second mourning. For Richardson, writing about Van Dyck's portrait of the Countess of Exeter *[fig.27]*, it was clear that she was portrayed as if 'receiving a Visit of Condolance from an Inferior with great Benignity', because had she been receiving her equals or superiors 'the Furniture of the Place must have been mourning, and her Gloves on'. How little we today know about mourning furniture! And how little about the etiquette of gloves – so obviously important in the history of portraiture.

The most elaborate meanings found in mourning were more commonly suspected than intended, but they could be intended and the Elizabethan poet Samuel Daniel, in the preface to his translation of Giovio's book of *Imprese* cites a love-crossed gentleman who, learning of the death of a friend's wife, went to a feast wearing

. . . blacke Grogran drawn out with Taffatie, and both cut on black Damaske, in such sort that the Damaske was best seen to be blackest–which mourning habit was no sooner seene of such as knewe the history of his love, but they perceived what it signified, as well as he himself had declared it–and greatly did they commend the invention.

The damask represented his own grief and was revealed as profounder than his grief for his friend, for his friend's wife was 'called to the heavens', but he stood 'secluded from the favour of a proud disdainefull dame'. It would be hard to communicate in this sort of way (supposing one wanted to be so impolite) in a society which did not have a rigid framework of sartorial conventions, against which the smallest variations and deviations become eloquent.

The advantages of well defined and widely shared conventions for the expression of grief are now perhaps quite as apparent as the absurdity and unpleasantness of the conventions which prevailed a hundred years ago. This does not only apply to dress. No one writing a letter of condolence, however sincere, could fail to regret the poverty of modern epistolary conventions. And it is hardly possible, when there is no tradition of dignified public language, to write an epitaph or elegy which is neither pompous nor whimsical. Psychoanalysis suggests that we need to mourn, as a sacrifice of a part of ourselves in penance for thoughts, not necessarily even conscious, which we directed against the deceased. Anthropologists are unlikely to discover any society which has dispensed with all mourning ritual. If the ritual must be performed, it is most easily performed when the suits of woe are prescribed and shared by our neighbours.

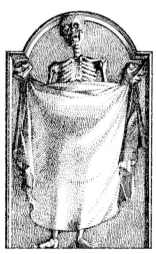

Bibliography

For a brief introduction to Chinese tomb figures see Edmund Capon's *Chinese Tomb Figures*, Victoria and Albert Small Colour Books, London (HMSO), 1976. Michael Loewe's *Everyday Life in Early Imperial China* places the sumptuous burial chambers of the Han period within the context of contemporary social structure and systems of belief. The full title of Thomas Greenhill's forgotten classic of 1705 is Νεκροκηδεια, *or The Art of Embalming*. A full report on the exhumation of the remains of Edward I was published in *Archaeologia* in 1786. For a discussion of whether or not Princess Charlotte should have been embalmed, see the anonymous *Life and Memoirs of her Royal Highness Princess Charlotte of Saxe Coburg, Saalfeld etc.*, published London, 1818, by T. Kinnersley. Chamber's projected mausoleum for Prince Frederick is discussed by John Harris in *Sir William Chambers*, London, 1970. For landscaped cemeteries see my article 'The Commercial Garden Necropolis of the Early Nineteenth Century and its Critics', *Garden History*, Summer 1974, John Morley's excellent *Death, Heaven and the Victorians*, London, 1971, chapters 3 and 4.

John Morley's book also contains the best account of the Victorian undertaker and his critics, and a good account of Wellington's funeral–but for this see also Michael Greenhalgh, 'The Funeral of the Duke of Wellington', *Apollo*, September 1973, and the account in Richard Redgrave, *A Memoir, Compiled from his Diary*, London 1891. For Nelson's funeral see my article 'The Obsequies of Nelson', *Country Life*, August 29, 1976. La Rochefoucauld's comments on English funerals will be found in his 'Mélanges' translated by S. C. Roberts as *A Frenchman in England, 1784*, Cambridge, 1933. The Sixteenth Century origins of spectacular funerals for European princes are discussed by Eve Borsook in 'Art and Politics at the Medici Court', *Mitteilungen des Kunsthistorischen Institute in Florenz*, 1965/6, 1966/7 and 1967/8. Allan Braham's *Funeral Decorations in Early Eighteenth Century Rome*, Victoria and Albert Museum Brochures no. VII, London (HMSO), 1965, traces later developments.

For Gregorio di Allegretto's shrine, and all other Italian sculpture discussed here, see the three volumes of the *Catalogue of the Italian Sculpture in the Victoria and Albert Museum* by Sir John Pope-Hennessy (assisted by R. Lightbrown), London, 1964. Shrines and Chantries, together with medieval altar tombs, are described, explained and illustrated by T. S. R. Boase in *Death in the Middle Ages*, London, 1972. Recumbent effigies and the Renaissance 'activation' of the effigy are discussed in Erwin Panofsky's *Tomb Sculpture*, London, 1964. The double tomb to Sir Moyle Finch and Elizabeth, Countess of Winchilsea, is explored in detail and convincingly ascribed to Nicholas Stone in John Physick's paper 'Five Monuments from Eastwell' in *The Victoria and Albert Museum Yearbook*, II, 1970. Stanton's drawing for the Brownlow monument is discussed, along with many other designs for monuments, by John Physick in *Designs for English Sculpture 1680–1860*, London (HMSO), 1969.

Rysbrack's sculpture is the subject of a fine monograph by M. I. Webb, *Michael Rysbrack*, London, 1954, and of Chapter 12 of Margaret Whinney's *Sculpture in Britain, 1530–1830*, Harmondsworth, 1964. For the terracotta Capponi bust see Pope-Hennessy's catalogue, already cited. For ways of representing decay, the dead and Death see the books by Boase and Panofsky, already cited, and for late eighteenth century sepulchral sculpture Hugh Honour's *Neo Classicism*, Harmondsworth, 1968, and my *Church Monuments in Romantic England*, London, 1977. The 23rd chapter of Margaret Whinney's *Sculpture in Britain* (see above) provides a good introduction to Flaxman's sculpture, and his models are fully catalogued by her and Rupert Gunnis in *The Collection of Models by John Flaxman R.A. at University College, London*, London, 1967.

Jonathan Richardson's passage on Van Dyck's portrait is a part of one of the most remarkable exercizes in art criticism in our language, to be found in *The Connoisseur*, one of *Two Discourses*, London, 1719 (republished 1972 in facsimile, by the Scolar Press). For Redgrave's paintings see his Memoir, cited earlier. For the mourning dress of the last century see Anne Buck's paper 'The Trap Re-Baited: Mourning Dress 1860–1890' in *High Victorian*, The Costume Society Spring Conference, 1968, and Chapter 6 of John Morley's *Death, Heaven and the Victorians*, cited earlier. For mourning dress in general see P. Cunnington and C. Lucas, *Costume for Births, Marriages and Deaths*, London, 1972. Samuel Daniel's 'englishing' of Giovio was published in 1585 as *The Worthy Tract of Paulus Iovius, containing a Discourse of rare inventions, both Militarie and Amorous called Imprese*.

Index

Printed in England for Her Majesty's Stationery Office by Balding + Mansell, Wisbech
Dd. 587527 K80